Doctor Faustus

Christopher Marlowe

Level 4

Retold by Chris Rice
Series Editors: Andy Hopkins and Jocelyn Potter

T0345395

Pearson Education Limited
Edinburgh Gate, Harlow,
Essex CM20 2JE, England
and Associated Companies throughout the world.

ISBN: 978-1-4058-6775-7

This edition first published 2008

10

Text copyright © Pearson Education Ltd 2008
Illustrations by George Sharp

Set in 11/14pt Bembo
Printed in China
SWTC/10

The authors have asserted their moral rights in accordance with the
Copyright Designs and Patents Act 1988.

Produced for the publishers by Ken Vail Graphic Design, Cambridge

*All rights reserved; no part of this publication may be reproduced, stored
in a retrieval system, or transmitted in any form or by any means,
electronic, mechanical, photocopying, recording or otherwise, without the
prior written permission of the Publishers.*

Published by Pearson Education Ltd

*Every effort has been made to trace the copyright holders and we apologise in advance for any unintentional omissions.
We would be pleased to insert the appropriate acknowledgement in any subsequent edition of this publication.*

For a complete list of the titles available in the Pearson English Readers series, please visit
www.pearsonenglishreaders.com.
Alternatively, write to your local Pearson Education office or to Pearson English Readers
Marketing Department, Pearson Education, Edinburgh Gate, Harlow, Essex CM20 2JE, England.

Contents

page

Introduction

'These books by magicians — lines, circles and mysterious drawings — yes, these are the books that I enjoy most. Oh, what a world of power and reward they promise the hard-working student! With this knowledge, I'll be master of everything that moves on Earth.'

These are the words of Doctor John Faustus, a famous scholar at the University of Wittenberg in Germany. He knows everything about philosophy, theology, law and medicine – but this knowledge is not enough. He wants more. He wants power over life itself, and is prepared to sign an agreement with the Devil to get it. In return for twenty-four years of magical power beyond most people's imagination, Faustus promises to give the Devil (Lucifer) his soul. At first, this seems an excellent agreement. With the help of Mephistopheles, Lucifer's loyal assistant, all Faustus's wishes come true. He learns the secrets of magic, brings famous people back from the dead, plays jokes on the Pope in Rome and makes his enemies grow horns. He can even produce fresh fruit in the middle of winter. But in his heart, Faustus is worried. Was it really a good idea to lose his soul forever in return for this earthly power? Why hasn't power, money and the admiration of others brought him happiness? As time passes, his desire to repent grows stronger. But is there any way that he can escape his final punishment of eternal damnation in hell?

Christopher Marlowe was an English actor and writer of poems and plays during the time of Queen Elizabeth I. He was born in 1564, the same year as William Shakespeare but, unlike Shakespeare, he went to university. Marlowe had a short but very eventful, and often mysterious, life. At first, when he finished his studies at Cambridge, the university refused to accept that he had passed his exams. They thought that he was a Catholic, and Catholicism was an illegal religion at that time. They changed their mind when they received a letter from the court of Queen Elizabeth, saying that Marlowe had 'done good service' for his queen and country. Many people now believe that Marlowe worked as a spy for the English government while he was a student.

Soon after he left Cambridge, Marlowe produced his first play for the London theatre, *Tamburlaine the Great* (1587). It appeared in two parts, and was an immediate success. Marlowe wrote five more plays, including *The Jew of Malta, Edward II* and *Doctor Faustus*. He was the first writer to write plays in the form of long poems. Many other writers, including Shakespeare, later used the same style.

In 1589, Marlowe spent three months in prison after he killed a man in a fight, but he was found not guilty of murder. After many other secret adventures in France and Holland and more trouble with the law in England, Marlowe was killed in a fight in East London on 30 May 1593, aged twenty-nine. Many people believe that the government had him murdered.

Doctor Faustus was probably written in 1592, a year before Marlowe died, but it was not performed until ten years later. Although the story had been told before, Marlowe's play is the first famous telling of the story. Since then, *Doctor Faustus* has become one of the most famous and powerful stories in world literature. Sometimes we all do bad things for power or money. There is a little bit of Doctor Faustus inside us all.

Reading and acting the play

You can read *Doctor Faustus* silently, like every other story in a book. You will have to imagine the places, people's clothes and their voices from the words on the page. But Christopher Marlowe did not write *Doctor Faustus* as literature for reading; he wrote it for actors on a stage. You can read the play in a group with other people, which is very different from silent reading. When you speak the words, you can bring the characters in the play to life. They can sound happy or sad, worried or angry. You can also stop and discuss the play. What does this person mean? Why does he or she say that?

But you can have even more fun if you act the play. Although *Doctor Faustus* does not have as much action as some other plays, it has a lot of emotional speeches and arguments. It has many exciting scenes as well as a few funny ones. You can have great fun dressing up as angels, devils or monks, or as famous historical characters like Alexander the Great and Helen of Troy.

You should think about the equipment and furniture that you will need in the different scenes. Many of the scenes take place in Faustus's study at the university, so you will need a lot of papers and books! But there are also scenes in dark woods and bright palaces, so you will need to show shadows and moonlight as well as bright lights and expensive chairs. You will need special equipment like knives, grapes, a bucket of burning wood, and big forks for the devils. You will also have fun with special effects: blood on Faustus's arm, shining eyes for the devils, people who grow horns, and thunder and lightning. Finally, the story covers twenty-four years, so Faustus and the other characters will need to grow older as the story progresses.

Doctor Faustus is a wonderful play. You can read it or act it but, most important of all, you can have fun and enjoy it!

The Characters in the Play

THE STORYTELLER

DOCTOR JOHN FAUSTUS
VALDES and CORNELIUS, Faustus's friends
THREE SCHOLARS
WAGNER, Faustus's servant
ROBIN, Wagner's follower
RAFE, Robin's friend

LUCIFER, the Devil
MEPHISTOPHELES, the Devil's helper

THE GOOD ANGEL
THE EVIL ANGEL
AN OLD MAN

THE POPE
THE CARDINAL OF LORRAINE
THE KING OF GERMANY
AN ARMY OFFICER
THE DUKE AND DUCHESS OF VANHOLT

PRIDE, COVETOUSNESS, ANGER, JEALOUSY, GREED, LAZINESS, LUST,
   the Seven Deadly Sins
ALEXANDER THE GREAT and his wife, HELEN OF TROY, spirits
TWO SEXY FEMALE DEVILS
SEVERAL MONKS
THE KING OF GERMANY'S SERVANTS
THREE DEVILS WITH LONG FORKS

Scene 1   The Storyteller Introduces the Story

[*The Storyteller enters and stands in front of the curtain.*]

STORYTELLER [*to the audience*]: In this story you will not hear about wars between great nations, about lovers in the courts of kings or about brave, heroic acts. We will perform only this: the story of a man named Faustus and his fortunes, good and bad. I must ask you to be patient as I tell you about his early life.

He was born into a poor family in Germany, in a town called Rhode. When he was older, he went to Wittenberg, where he studied and became a doctor of theology. No one was cleverer than he was, but he was too proud of his gifts. With paper wings he flew too near the sun, and heaven planned his downfall. Drunk with the greatness of his knowledge and ability, he became too interested in the power of the Devil. To him, now, there is nothing as sweet as the Devil's magic; it has become his greatest pleasure. This is the man that we now see in his study.

[*The Storyteller leaves. The curtain goes up.*]

Scene 2   Faustus Makes a Decision

[*Faustus's study. Faustus is sitting at his desk in a shadowy room filled with books, papers, and glass bottles containing strange-coloured liquids.*]

FAUSTUS [*talking to himself with a look of thoughtful worry on his face*]: You have to make a decision about your studies, Faustus. You must discover how deep your knowledge really is. You've started well and you seem very wise, but at the end of every road you find Aristotle. [*He picks up a book and smiles.*] Sweet Aristotle, you've filled me with so much happiness. [*reading*]

'The aim of philosophy is to discuss things well.' [*He looks up and shakes his head.*] Is that all? Is the aim of philosophy simply to produce a good argument? Is that the greatest miracle that this art has to offer? If it is, Faustus, then read no more. You've already succeeded in your aim. Your mind demands a greater challenge. Say goodbye to philosophy. [*He pushes the book away and picks up another book.*]

Where philosophy ends, medicine begins. Be a doctor, Faustus. Make mountains of gold and become famous forever by finding a miracle cure. [*He reads from the second book.*] 'The aim of medicine is our body's health.' [*He looks up and again shakes his head with annoyance.*] Haven't you already succeeded in that area, Faustus? You know everything about medicine, and the world listens to your advice. You've saved whole cities from terrible illnesses and cured a thousand diseases. But you're still Faustus, and you're still only a man. If you could make men live for ever, or bring dead men back to life, that would be *real* success. So, goodbye to medicine. [*He pushes the second book away and impatiently looks for a third.*]

Where's the book of Roman law? [*He finds it and reads.*] 'If two people want the same thing, one should have the thing itself, the other should have its value … ' [*He pushes the book away and sits back in his chair with a sigh.*] A perfect example of meaninglessness. The law might be all right for small-minded men who are only interested in money. But it's too dull for me. Perhaps theology is best. [*He sits up and opens a fourth book.*]

The Bible, Faustus – read it well. [*reading*] 'The reward of sin is death.' [*laughing*] Ha! That's cruel. [*reading*] 'If we say that we have no sin, we are lying to ourselves.' [*amused*] We all sin. Is that why we must all die and be dead forever? [*suddenly angry*] What teaching do you call this? What will be, will be? [*He pushes the book away.*] Goodbye, theology! [*He picks up a book of magic and his face softens.*]

These books by magicians – lines, circles and mysterious drawings – yes, these are the books that I enjoy most. Oh, what a world of power and reward they promise the hard-working student! With this knowledge, I'll be master of everything that moves on Earth. Kings are only obeyed in their own countries; they can't command the winds or control the clouds. But if a man can master this [*waving the book in his hands*], his power will stretch as far as his imagination. A good magician is a powerful god. [*smiling with excitement*] This is your answer, Faustus. Use your brain and become a god.

[*He stands up and calls his servant.*] Wagner! [*Wagner enters.*] Ask my dearest friends, Valdes and Cornelius, to visit me immediately.

WAGNER: I will, sir. [*He leaves.*]

FAUSTUS: Their advice will be a greater help to me than hard work on my own.

[*Two Angels enter: the Good Angel, dressed in white, from the right; the Evil Angel, dressed in black, from the left.*]

GOOD ANGEL [*angrily*]: Oh, Faustus, put that evil book away. If you look at it, it will tempt your soul and bring the power of God's anger down on you. Read the Bible instead.

EVIL ANGEL [*with a cruel smile*]: Yes, Faustus, study the art of magic and discover all nature's mysteries. Be as powerful on Earth as God is in the sky – be lord and commander of all these secrets.

[*The Angels leave.*]

Scene 3 The Excitement of Magic

[*Faustus's study*]

FAUSTUS [*excited*]: These thoughts fill me with such hungry desire! Will spirits fetch me whatever I want, solve every mystery and do whatever I ask them? I'll tell them to fly to India for gold, to search the ocean floor for treasure and to go to every corner of the new-found world for pleasant fruits and tempting sweets. I'll make them read strange philosophy to me and tell me the secrets of all foreign kings. I'll make them build a wall of iron around Germany and make the River Rhine circle fair Wittenberg. I'll make them dress all university students in the finest clothes. I'll buy an army with the money that they bring me. I'll be the king of all our land. I'll command my spirits to invent new instruments of war ...

[*calling loudly*] Come, Valdes and Cornelius, give me your wise advice! [*Valdes and Cornelius enter.*] Valdes, sweet Valdes, and Cornelius, your words have finally led me to practise magic and the secret arts – not only your words, but my own dreams. Philosophy is hateful and complicated; both law and medicine are for small-minded men; theology is the worst of them all – unpleasant, cruel, stupid and ugly. It's magic that excites me. So, gentle friends, if you help me in this adventure, I, with my excellent mind, will become the world's greatest magician.

VALDES [*pleased*]: Faustus, these books, your intelligence and our experience will make us world famous. In the same way that servants obey their lords, the spirits of the magical world will serve us three. They'll guard us whenever we choose; they'll be as brave as German horsemen or more beautiful than angels. They'll bring us treasure from Venice and ships full of gold from America – if wise Faustus has a strong enough desire.

FAUSTUS: Valdes, have no fear. My desire for this is as strong as your desire to live.

4

'These thoughts fill me with such hungry desire!'

CORNELIUS [*enthusiastically*]: You'll have no wish to study anything else when you see the miracles that magic will perform. If you've studied the stars, languages and science, you'll easily master the laws of magic. The spirits tell me that they can dry the sea and fetch treasure from ships at the bottom of every ocean – yes, all the riches that our fathers have hidden below the earth.

FAUSTUS [*smiling*]: Oh, this excites my soul! [*urgently*] You must show me examples of this magic. I want to practise it and discover its mysterious pleasures for myself.

VALDES: We'll find a secret place and show you how it works.

CORNELIUS [*to Valdes*]: First, let him know the secret words. Then, when he's learnt what to do, he'll be able to try it by himself.

VALDES [*to Faustus*]: After I've taught you how to start, you'll soon be better at it than I am.

FAUSTUS [*putting his arms around their shoulders*]: Then come and have dinner with me. Afterwards, we'll study it in every detail. Tonight, I'll perform magic, even if I die trying.

[*They leave.*]

Scene 4 Two Scholars Fear for Faustus

[*A room in the university. Two Scholars are sitting in chairs by a fire.*]

FIRST SCHOLAR: I wonder what's happened to Faustus? The university used to be filled with his loud voice arguing about philosophy.

SECOND SCHOLAR: We'll soon find out. Here comes his servant.

[*Wagner enters, carrying wine.*]

FIRST SCHOLAR [*to Wagner*]: Tell me, young man, where's your master?

WAGNER [*with a sigh*]: God in heaven knows.

SECOND SCHOLAR [*surprised*]: What? And you *don't* know?

WAGNER: Yes, *I* know. But that doesn't mean much.

FIRST SCHOLAR [*annoyed*]: Don't be foolish, young man. Tell us where he is.

WAGNER [*playfully serious, like a teacher*]: Scholars like you should be more thoughtful. Recognise your mistake and pay more attention.

SECOND SCHOLAR [*confused*]: I thought you said that you *knew*.

WAGNER [*wide-eyed with innocence*]: Have you any witnesses?

FIRST SCHOLAR [*angrily*]: Yes — *I* heard you!

WAGNER [*with a knowing smile*]: Yes, thieves always support each other.

SECOND SCHOLAR [*turning away, refusing to let Wagner's rudeness make him angry*]: So you aren't going to tell us?

WAGNER: No, sir, I *will* tell you. But intelligent men shouldn't need to ask questions like this. My master's human, isn't he? And humans can move from place to place, can't they? So why are you asking such meaningless questions? If I weren't such a calm, relaxed person, I wouldn't even enter into conversation with people like you. But as I've already won the argument, I'll be serious and tell you where he is. He's having dinner with Valdes and Cornelius. This wine in my hand, if it could speak, would tell you the same. And now, my good lords, my wise scholars, I must leave you. [*Wagner makes fun of the Scholars by lowering his head with extra politeness, and leaves.*]

FIRST SCHOLAR [*looking at the Second Scholar and shaking his head at this news*]: If he's with *them*, I fear that he's practising the evil art of magic. Valdes and Cornelius are well known for it around the world.

SECOND SCHOLAR: I'd pity him even if he weren't my colleague. [*standing up*] But come, let's inform the head of the university. Perhaps he, with his wise advice, can save Faustus.

FIRST SCHOLAR [*not moving from his chair*]: I'm afraid that nothing will save him.

SECOND SCHOLAR: But we can still try.

[*The Second Scholar leaves, followed unwillingly by the First Scholar.*]

Scene 5 Faustus Calls Mephistopheles

[*It is night time in a shadowy wood. Lamps are burning around the outside of a large white circle that Faustus has drawn on the ground. Faustus is walking around the circle. He is nervously excited, looking at the darkness surrounding him.*]

FAUSTUS [*talking to himself*]: Night's beginning to cover the sky with shadow, so, Faustus, you can begin your magic spells. Everything's prepared. Inside this circle, God's name has been written forwards and backwards. There are signs for all the stars that control the movements of spirits. Don't be afraid, therefore, Faustus – be brave, and see what magic you can perform. [*Faustus picks up a cup, puts his fingers inside it and throws drops of water over his face and body. At the same time he makes the sign of the cross with his hand, looks up at the sky and speaks slowly and loudly.*] Let the gods of hell be good to me. Let the God of heaven disappear. I greet you, spirits of fire, air and water. I greet you, Lucifer, the Prince of Darkness, the king of burning hell. Send me your servant, Mephistopheles, and let me speak to him. [*He pauses, but nothing happens.*]
What's the delay? [*He throws more water over his head and body and makes another sign of the cross.*] With this water and with these signs, I command Mephistopheles to appear! [*An ugly shape appears out of the shadows. It is dressed completely in black, and only its shining red eyes can be seen. Faustus, though, is not afraid. He points at the shape and shouts.*] I order you to go away and change your shape. You're too ugly to serve me! Go, and return as a monk. You'd look better like that. [*The shape walks*

8

slowly backwards into the shadows. Faustus smiles, pleased with his success.] I see that my heavenly words are working! This art is simple – anyone could do it! And how easy it is to control the Devil's servant! He obeys every command without a word. There's true power in this magic and my spells. [*He stands up straight and looks proudly up at the sky.*] Now, Faustus, you are a master of these magic arts. You can command the Devil's servant himself! [*He makes another sign of the cross and speaks slowly and loudly.*] Return immediately, Mephistopheles – but this time, come as a monk!

[*Mephistopheles, dressed as an old man in monk's clothes, appears slowly out of the shadows.*]

MEPHISTOPHELES: Now, Faustus, what would you like me to do?

FAUSTUS: I order you to serve me for as long as I live, and to do whatever I command. If I want the moon to fall from the sky or the oceans to cover the world, you'll do it.

MEPHISTOPHELES: I'm only the Devil's servant. I can't obey you without his permission. I can only perform what the Devil allows.

FAUSTUS [*surprised and confused*]: Didn't he command you to come here?

MEPHISTOPHELES: No, he doesn't know I'm here.

FAUSTUS: Didn't my magic spells bring you here?

MEPHISTOPHELES: Yes, but there was another reason for me to come. When I hear somebody attacking God's name or criticising his son, Jesus Christ, I fly in hope of winning his soul. The quickest way to call me is to challenge God and to show admiration for the Prince of Hell.

FAUSTUS [*thoughtfully*]: I've already done that, and I truly believe that the Devil is my only master. Punishment in hell doesn't frighten me. [*with more energy*] But let's forget about these unimportant things. Tell me about your lord, the Devil. What's he like?

9

MEPHISTOPHELES: He's the commander of all spirits.

FAUSTUS: Wasn't he an angel in the past?

MEPHISTOPHELES: Yes, Faustus, and he was loved dearly by God.

FAUSTUS: So how did he become the prince of devils?

MEPHISTOPHELES: He became proud and wanted too much power, so God threw him out of heaven.

FAUSTUS: And who else works for the Devil?

MEPHISTOPHELES: Unhappy spirits that were thrown out of heaven with him. They all suffer eternal punishment together.

FAUSTUS: Where is this eternal punishment?

MEPHISTOPHELES: In hell.

FAUSTUS: So how are you allowed to leave hell like this?

MEPHISTOPHELES [*opening his arms and looking around him*]: Hell is everywhere and I'm never out of it. [*looking sadly at Faustus*] I've seen the face of God and tasted the eternal happiness of heaven. Do you think that I didn't suffer when I lost that happiness? Oh, Faustus, forget these silly demands of yours. They fill my soul with fear!

FAUSTUS [*laughing at Mephistopheles's seriousness*]: Why is the great Mephistopheles so upset about losing the pleasures of heaven? Learn from my example – be brave, and forget about things that will never be yours. Take this message to your master: Faustus is already facing eternal death for attacking God's name. Say that I, Faustus, offer him my soul in return for twenty-four years of life with you as my servant. You'll give me whatever I ask for. You'll kill my enemies, help my friends and obey all my commands. Return to your master, and come to my study at midnight with his reply.

MEPHISTOPHELES [*unenthusiastically*]: I will, Faustus.

[*Mephistopheles walks backwards and disappears into the shadows.*]

FAUSTUS [*walking up and down with increasing excitement*]: If I had as many souls as there are stars, I'd give them all for

Mephistopheles. With his help, I'll rule the world; I'll build a bridge across the ocean and cross it with my men; I'll join the hills of the African shore to the coast of Spain, and both will be in my power; kings will only act with my permission ... [*relaxing, with a smile*] But while I'm waiting for Mephistopheles to return, I'll think carefully about how to use the powers that will soon be mine. [*He leaves.*]

Scene 6 Robin Becomes a Follower of Wagner

[*A kitchen in the university. Robin, a cheerful but poorly dressed young man with a small, pointed beard, is sitting by a fire. Wagner enters.*]

WAGNER: Boy, come here.

ROBIN [*offended*]: Boy? Why do you call me 'boy'? How many boys have you seen with pointed beards like mine?

WAGNER: Tell me, young man, are you earning any money?

ROBIN [*jokingly*]: Of course I am. [*He shows Wagner the holes in his clothes and shoes.*] Look how well I'm dressed.

WAGNER [*with a smile of amused pity*]: Poor boy. I see that you can still laugh, although you have no clothes. But you badly need work, I know. And you're so hungry that you'd give your soul to the Devil for a piece of meat, even if it was uncooked.

ROBIN [*playfully offended*]: What? Give my soul to the Devil for a piece of uncooked meat? Not true, my good friend. For such a high price, it would have to be very well cooked!

WAGNER: Well, if you worked for me, your situation would improve.

ROBIN [*interested*]: In what way?

WAGNER: Beautiful clothes and sweet-smelling soap.

ROBIN [*holding his nose and laughing*]: If I worked for you, I'd

11

certainly need plenty of soap!

WAGNER: You need it whether you work for me or not. But be serious for a minute, young man. If you serve me for seven years, you'll be well rewarded. [*He takes a few coins from a bag on his belt and offers them to Robin.*] Take these.

ROBIN [*taking the coins and looking at them uncertainly*]: And what do I have to do to earn these?

WAGNER: Serve the Devil whenever he calls you.

ROBIN [*interested*]: If I serve you, will you teach me to call devils?

WAGNER: I'll teach you to turn yourself into a dog, a cat, a mouse, a rat – whatever you like.

ROBIN: What? Would a Christian man turn into a dog, a cat, a mouse or a rat? No, no, sir. If you turn me into anything, let it be a very small insect. Then I could go wherever I liked and no one would see me.

WAGNER: Follow me. [*He begins to walk away.*]

ROBIN [*not moving*]: Did you hear me, Wagner?

WAGNER [*suddenly serious*]: Boy, you must call me *Master* Wagner, and never take your eyes off the back of my feet. You must follow every one of my footsteps. [*He turns away and leaves.*]

ROBIN: God forgive me, but I'll have to follow and serve him. There's no other way. [*He follows Wagner.*]

Scene 7   Faustus Has Doubts

[*Faustus is walking up and down nervously in his study. He is having doubts about what he is doing.*]

FAUSTUS [*anxiously to himself*]: Now, Faustus, do you really want eternal punishment? God can still save you ... [*shaking his head suddenly*] Away with such meaningless thoughts! Forget God and believe in the Devil. Don't be weak. No, Faustus, be brave. [*suddenly thoughtful*] But why do you have such doubts? Oh, there's a voice inside my head that tells me: 'Stop this magic, turn to God again.' [*He seems suddenly certain.*] Yes, Faustus *will* turn to God again. [*A look of doubt clouds his face.*] But, Faustus, why God? God doesn't love you. Your *desire* is the only God that *you* serve. And your desire has only one love: the Devil. [*smiling cruelly*] I'll build a church for him and offer him the warm blood of new-born babies.

[*The Good Angel enters from the right and the Evil Angel enters from the left.*]

GOOD ANGEL: Sweet Faustus, leave that diseased art of magic.
FAUSTUS: If I do, I'll need to show guilt and repentance.
GOOD ANGEL: They're roads that will lead you to heaven.
EVIL ANGEL: No, that's a lie. They're the fruits of madness. If you believe in *them*, you're a fool.
GOOD ANGEL: Sweet Faustus, think of heavenly things.
EVIL ANGEL: No, Faustus, think of power and money.

[*The Angels leave.*]

FAUSTUS [*smiling*]: Money? I'll be the richest man in the world! With Mephistopheles by my side, God can't hurt me. I'm safe. So, forget your doubts, Faustus. Come, Mephistopheles, and bring good news from your master. [*impatiently*] Isn't it midnight yet? Come, Mephistopheles! [*Mephistopheles appears, again dressed as a monk.*] Now tell me, what does Lucifer say?
MEPHISTOPHELES: He says that I should serve Faustus, and that Faustus will buy my service with his soul.
FAUSTUS [*impatiently*]: But I've already agreed to that.
MEPHISTOPHELES: But Faustus, you must make a formal promise. [*He produces a document from the pocket of his monk's clothes.*] You must write an official agreement with your blood. [*He sees Faustus pause uncertainly.*] If you refuse, I'll return to hell. [*He turns to leave.*]

FAUSTUS [*anxiously*]: No, wait, Mephistopheles. [*Mephistopheles stops.*] Tell me – what good will my soul do your master?

MEPHISTOPHELES: It will increase his power.

FAUSTUS: Is that why he tempts me like this?

MEPHISTOPHELES: Unhappy people enjoy the company of other unhappy people. Now tell me, Faustus, do you agree to give me your soul? Then I'll be your servant and bring you things beyond your imagination.

FAUSTUS [*after thinking for a moment*]: Yes, Mephistopheles, I agree.

Scene 8   Faustus Signs an Agreement

[*Faustus's study*]

MEPHISTOPHELES [*opening the document on Faustus's desk, producing a small knife from his pocket and offering it to Faustus*] Cut your arm bravely and write the agreement with your blood. On a certain day in the future, Great Lucifer will take your soul. But until that day, you'll be as powerful as he is.

FAUSTUS [*taking the knife and cutting his arm*]: Look, Mephistopheles, I'm cutting my arm for you. And with my own blood, I promise that Lucifer will have my soul. Great Lord and Master of eternal night, see the blood that's running from my arm. Let it prove to you that my desire is serious.

MEPHISTOPHELES [*offering Faustus a pen*]: But Faustus, you must write your agreement with it.

FAUSTUS [*taking the pen*]: Of course. [*He touches his blood with the pen and begins writing on the document. Suddenly, he looks up, confused.*] But Mephistopheles, my blood has gone dry. I can't write any more.

MEPHISTOPHELES: I'll find you some fire to warm it. [*He leaves.*]

FAUSTUS [*anxiously*]: What might this drying of my blood mean? Is it unwilling for me to write the agreement? Why has it

'And with my own blood, I promise that Lucifer will have my soul.'

stopped running? Am I supposed to start again? [*reading*] 'Faustus gives you his soul' – that's where it stopped! [*annoyed*] But why shouldn't I give away my soul? Doesn't my own soul belong to me? Never mind. I'll simply have to write it again – 'Faustus gives you his soul'.

[*Mephistopheles enters, carrying a bucket of burning wood.*]

MEPHISTOPHELES [*holding the bucket under Faustus's arm*]: Here's fire. Come Faustus, warm your arm with it.

FAUSTUS [*looking carefully at his arm above the bucket*] So, now the blood's beginning to run again. I'll finish the agreement immediately. [*He wets the pen with the blood from his arm and begins writing again.*]

MEPHISTOPHELES [*to the audience*]: I'll do anything to own his soul.

FAUSTUS [*lifting his pen from the document with a smile*]: It's done. Faustus has promised his soul to Lucifer. [*He looks at his arm.*] But what's this, written in blood on my arm? [*reading*] 'Run away, man!' [*looking up with surprise*] But where should I run away to? If I ran to God, he'd throw me down into hell. [*shaking his head with an embarrassed smile*] No, I'm imagining things. There's nothing written on my arm. [*He looks at his arm again and his smile disappears.*] No, I can see it clearly. It says, 'Run away, man!' [*looking up angrily*] But I refuse to run away!

MEPHISTOPHELES [*to the audience*]: I'll fetch him something to make him more cheerful.

[*He leaves and returns with two sexy Female Devils, who give Faustus some jewels and beautiful clothes. While Faustus admires the gifts, they perform a short dance and leave.*]

FAUSTUS [*with a confused smile*]: Tell me, Mephistopheles, what does this mean?

MEPHISTOPHELES: Nothing, Faustus. It's only something to bring you pleasure and to show you what magic can do.

FAUSTUS: But can I call spirits whenever I want?

MEPHISTOPHELES: Yes, and you can do even greater things than that.

FAUSTUS [*happily*]: Then that's enough for a thousand souls. [*picking up the document*] Here, Mephistopheles, take this document promising to give you my body and soul. You must, though, do everything for me that we've agreed.

MEPHISTOPHELES [*putting his hand on his heart*]: I promise, Faustus, in the name of hell and Lucifer, to keep all the promises that we've made between us.

FAUSTUS: Then let me read them to you. [*Opening the document, he reads.*] 'I, Doctor John Faustus of Wittenberg, promise with this document to give both body and soul to Lucifer, Prince of the East, and his minister, Mephistopheles. I give them full permission, twenty-four years from today, to fetch or carry John Faustus, body and soul, to any place of their choice, if the following conditions have been met:

FIRST, Mephistopheles will be Faustus's servant and obey every command that he makes.

SECOND, Mephistopheles will do for him and bring him whatever he asks for.

THIRD, only Faustus will be able to see Mephistopheles.

FINALLY, Mephistopheles will appear at all times in whatever shape or form that Faustus desires.

Signed, by me, John Faustus.'

MEPHISTOPHELES: Tell me, Faustus, is this your final agreement?

FAUSTUS [*giving Mephistopheles the document*]: Yes. Take it, and let the Devil do his work.

Scene 9 Faustus Makes His First Requests

[*Faustus's study*]

MEPHISTOPHELES [*putting the document in the pocket of his monk's clothes*]: Now, Faustus, what's your first request?

FAUSTUS: I want to ask you first about hell. Tell me, where is it?

MEPHISTOPHELES: Under the heavens.

FAUSTUS: Yes, but where exactly?

MEPHISTOPHELES: In the heart of everything, where we suffer and live forever. Hell has no limits. It isn't found in just one place. Wherever we are, hell can be found. Wherever hell is, we must be. When the world ends, hell will be everywhere that is not heaven.

FAUSTUS [*laughing*]: I don't believe that hell exists.

MEPHISTOPHELES [*with a sigh*]: You can believe that if you like, until experience changes your mind.

FAUSTUS: Do you think that Faustus will be eternally damned?

MEPHISTOPHELES: Of course. [*He touches the pocket containing the agreement.*] This document proves that your soul now belongs to Lucifer.

FAUSTUS: I know. My soul *and* body. But what does *that* matter? Do I honestly believe that after this life there's any pain? [*laughing again*] No, that's only a story invented to frighten children.

MEPHISTOPHELES: But, Faustus, I'm here to prove the opposite. I'm damned and am now in hell.

FAUSTUS [*with disbelief*]: How are *you* now in hell? [*He points around at his study.*] If this is hell, I'll happily be damned here. Walking, arguing and talking doesn't seem frightening to me. [*suddenly serious*] But let's forget all that for a minute. Let me have a wife, the most beautiful woman in Germany. I'm hungry for love and can't live without a wife.

MEPHISTOPHELES [*surprised*]: A wife? I strongly advise you, Faustus, not to have a wife.

18

FAUSTUS: No, sweet Mephistopheles, fetch me one immediately. I want one now.

MEPHISTOPHELES [*sighing again*]: Well, if that's what you want, I'll fetch you one in the Devil's name. Sit there while I find you one. [*Faustus sits down while Mephistopheles leaves. Mephistopheles returns a few seconds later with a Devil dressed like a woman but with an ugly painted face. She smiles sexily at Faustus.*] Tell me, Faustus, how do you like your wife?

FAUSTUS [*looking sick*]: Take her away! She's horrible!

MEPHISTOPHELES [*smiling playfully*]: But Faustus, marriage is only a meaningless toy. If you love me, think no more about it. [*The Devil leaves.*] I'll find the most beautiful women in the land for you and bring them every morning to your bed. You'll win the heart of whoever you like best, whether she's young and pure, old and wise, or as beautiful as Lucifer was before his downfall.

[*He takes an old book from inside his clothes and shows it to Faustus.*] Take this book and read it carefully. [*He opens the book at a page and shows it to Faustus.*] These lines, for example, will bring you gold. [*turning to another page and showing it*] If you draw this circle on the ground, there'll be wild winds, thunder and lightning. [*turning to another page and showing it*] If you say these words three times quietly to yourself, an army of soldiers will obey every command you give.

FAUSTUS [*taking the book and looking through it enthusiastically, like a child*]: Thanks, Mephistopheles. But I'd really love to have a book containing *all* the world's spells. Then I'd be able to call up spirits whenever I wanted.

MEPHISTOPHELES [*taking the book, opening it and showing it to Faustus.*]: They're all in this book. Look.

FAUSTUS: I'd also like a book that showed me the position and secret meaning of all the stars in heaven.

MEPHISTOPHELES [*turning to another page*]: The stars are all in here, too.

19

FAUSTUS [*with a challenging smile*]: Then let me have a book where I might learn about all the world's plants and trees.

MEPHISTOPHELES [*turning to another page*]: Here they are.

FAUSTUS [*staring at Mephistopheles with admiration and disbelief*]: You must be joking.

MEPHISTOPHELES [*returning the book to Faustus with a mysterious smile*]: I promise you I'm not.

[*They leave.*]

Scene 10   Robin Makes Plans

[*Robin is sitting by the fire in the university kitchen, looking at a book.*]

ROBIN [*smiling proudly and talking to himself*]: Oh, this is wonderful! I've stolen one of Doctor Faustus's books and I'm going to find some magic spells for *me* to use. I'll make all the pretty young girls around here take off their clothes and dance for me. I'll see more than I've ever seen before!

[*Rafe, a friend of Robin's, enters the kitchen.*]

RAFE [*noticing the book*]: What are you doing with that book?

ROBIN: It's the greatest book of magic spells ever invented by the Devil.

RAFE [*interested*]: Can you work this magic?

ROBIN: With this book, I can easily do anything. I can make you as drunk as a lord, and you won't have to pay a penny. [*He stands up, puts his arm around Rafe's shoulders and speaks softly.*] Or, if you're interested in Nan Spit, the cook's pretty young assistant, you can have her. Whenever you like! Even at midnight!

RAFE [*excitedly*]: Oh, clever Robin! Can I really have Nan Spit as often as I like?

ROBIN [*putting his finger to his lips*]: Not so loud, sweet Rafe. Let's go and try some of this devil's magic!

[*They leave.*]

Scene 11 Faustus's Doubts Return

[*Faustus enters his study with Mephistopheles.*]

FAUSTUS [*unhappily*]: When I look at the heavens, I repent my sins. I'm angry with you for tempting me, Mephistopheles, and for taking away my happiness.

MEPHISTOPHELES [*calmly*]: Is heaven really so wonderful? I promise you, it's not half as wonderful as you or any other man that breathes on this earth.

FAUSTUS [*with a challenging look*]: Prove it!

MEPHISTOPHELES: Heaven was made for man, so man must therefore be more excellent.

FAUSTUS: If heaven was made for man, then it was made for me. I'll stop this magic immediately and repent.

[*The Good Angel and the Evil Angel enter.*]

GOOD ANGEL: Repent, Faustus, and God will pity you.

EVIL ANGEL: You're a spirit, so God can't pity you.

FAUSTUS [*angry and confused, to himself*]: What voice inside my head is telling me that I'm a spirit? God would pity me even if I were a devil. Yes, God *will* pity me if I repent.

EVIL ANGEL [*with cruel amusement*]: Yes, but Faustus will never repent.

[*The Angels leave.*]

FAUSTUS [*sadly to himself*]: My heart's so hard that I can't repent. I only have to think of the word 'heaven' and I hear a voice thundering in my ears: 'Faustus, you are damned!' Then knives,

21

guns and poison appear in front of me, tempting me to use them against myself. And I'd gladly kill myself – [*suddenly smiling*] but sweet pleasure destroys my darkest sadness. Great writers from the past have read their poems to me. Singers from a thousand years ago have filled my ears with their beautiful music. Why should I die, then? Why should I feel guilty? I promise that Faustus will never repent. [*to Mephistopheles*] Come, Mephistopheles, let's talk again about science. Tell me, who made the world?

MEPHISTOPHELES: I will not.

FAUSTUS: Sweet Mephistopheles, tell me.

MEPHISTOPHELES: Don't ask, because I won't tell you.

FAUSTUS [*angrily*]: Haven't you promised to answer any question that I ask?

MEPHISTOPHELES: Only if it's of no danger to my master. Limit your thoughts to hell, Faustus, because you're damned. [*He leaves.*]

FAUSTUS [*shouting angrily*]: Yes, go, you evil spirit, to ugly hell! You're the one who's damned poor Faustus's soul! [*He turns away with his head in his hands.*] It isn't too late to be saved, is it?

[*The Good Angel and the Evil Angel enter.*]

EVIL ANGEL: It's too late.

GOOD ANGEL: It's never too late, if Faustus can repent.

EVIL ANGEL: If you repent, devils will tear you to pieces.

GOOD ANGEL: Repent, and devils will never harm you.

[*The Angels leave.*]

FAUSTUS [*falling to his knees and lifting his face and hands to the sky*]: Christ, save poor Faustus's soul!

'Christ, save poor Faustus's soul!'

Scene 12   Faustus Meets the Seven Deadly Sins

[*Mephistopheles enters Faustus's study with Lucifer, his master – the Devil.*]

LUCIFER: Christ can't save your soul. No one's interested in your soul except me.

FAUSTUS [*still on his knees, staring at Lucifer*]: And who are you?

LUCIFER: I'm Lucifer.

FAUSTUS [*frightened, to himself*]: Oh, Faustus, he's come to take away your soul!

LUCIFER: I've come to tell you that you've insulted me. You've been talking about Christ, which is against the rules of our agreement. You shouldn't think about Christ. Think only of the Devil.

FAUSTUS [*holding his hands together and looking at the ground*]: Forgive me. I promise never to think about heaven or talk about God again.

LUCIFER: Good. [*smiling warmly*] But don't worry, Faustus. I've come from hell to offer you some entertainment. Sit down, and the Seven Deadly Sins will visit you.

FAUSTUS [*standing up and moving towards a chair*]: I'll enjoy this very much! [*He sits down.*]

[*The Seven Deadly Sins enter.*]

LUCIFER: Now, Faustus, examine them and learn their different characters.

FAUSTUS: Who are you, the first one?

PRIDE: I'm Pride. I have no parents. I can hide, like dust, in every corner of a woman's body. Sometimes I can sit in her hair, at other times I can kiss her on the lips. I can go anywhere I please. [*He looks down, pulls a face and puts a handkerchief to his nose.*] But what's that terrible smell? I refuse to say another word until the floor's covered with a better-quality carpet.

FAUSTUS: And who's the second one?

COVETOUSNESS: I'm Covetousness. I was born inside an old money bag, the child of rude, unintelligent parents. If I had one wish, I'd like everyone and everything in this house to turn into gold. Then I'd lock you all up in my treasure box. Oh, sweet gold!

FAUSTUS: And what about you, number three?

ANGER: I'm Anger. I had no parents. I jumped out of a wild animal's mouth when I was half an hour old. Since then, I've run up and down the world [*He holds up a bag and shakes it.*] with this bag of sharp knives. If I have no one to fight, I fight myself.

FAUSTUS: Who's the fourth one?

JEALOUSY: I'm Jealousy. My father was a chimney-sweep and my mother a fish-seller. I can't read, and would therefore like all books to be burnt. I'm thin from watching others eat. I'd be happy if there was no more food in the world and everyone died of hunger. Then you'd see how fat I could be. [*He moves towards Faustus.*] But why are you sitting when I have to stand? Stand up immediately!

FAUSTUS [*pushing Jealousy away*]: Away, you jealous animal! [*He turns to the fifth Deadly Sin.*]: And who are you, number five?

GREED: I'm Greed. My parents are both dead, and they've only left me enough money for thirty meals a day. Oh, my family's truly royal. My grandfather was a mountain of meat, my grandmother was a lake of wine. My uncle was a jar of fish and my aunt – such a cheerful, popular woman! – was a large bottle of beer. Now, Faustus, you've heard all about my family – will you invite me to supper?

FAUSTUS: I'd prefer to see you dead. You'd eat everything in the house.

GREED [*angrily*]: I hope the Devil sticks in your throat!

FAUSTUS: Stick in your own throat, you fat devil! [*He turns to the sixth Deadly Sin.*] Tell me about yourself, number six.

LAZINESS: I'm Laziness. I was born in a sunny field, where I've lived ever since. [*annoyed*] And you've seriously offended me by calling me away from there! I want Greed and Lust to carry me back. I refuse to say another word until they do!

FAUSTUS: And who are you, the seventh and final one?

LUST [*in a low, sexy voice*]: I'm Lust. I prefer my meat uncooked, and before I eat it I like to kiss it.

LUCIFER [*waving the Seven Deadly Sins away*]: Go back to hell, all of you! [*The Deadly Sins leave.*] [*to Faustus*] Now, Faustus, do you like the Seven Deadly Sins?

FAUSTUS [*excitedly*]: Oh, they feed my soul!

LUCIFER [*smiling*]: There's even more pleasure than this in hell.

FAUSTUS: If I could see hell and return again, I'd be so happy!

LUCIFER: You will. I'll send for you at midnight. [*He gives Faustus a book.*] While you're waiting, take this book and read it carefully. Then you'll be able to turn yourself into whatever shape you like.

FAUSTUS [*taking the book gratefully*]: Many thanks, great Lucifer. I'll guard this with my life.

LUCIFER: Goodbye, Faustus, and think about the Devil.

FAUSTUS: Goodbye, great Lucifer. [*to Mephistopheles*] Come, Mephistopheles.

[*Faustus and Mephistopheles sit at the desk and open the book as Lucifer leaves. The curtain falls.*]

Scene 13 The Storyteller Introduces the Next Part of the Story

[*The Storyteller enters and stands in front of the curtain.*]

STORYTELLER [*to the audience*]: Wise Faustus wanted to discover the secrets of the stars, so he climbed to the top of Mount Olympus, the home of the old Greek gods. He has now taken his maps of the heavens away – to Rome. There, he will meet the Pope and will perhaps enjoy taking part in the St Peter's Day celebrations.

[*The Storyteller leaves and the curtain goes up.*]

Scene 14 Faustus Amuses Himself in the Pope's Palace

[*Faustus and Mephistopheles enter a large room in the Pope's palace in Rome.*]

FAUSTUS: You've shown me, Mephistopheles, the deep lakes and enormous mountains surrounding the old German city of Trier. After Paris, you showed me the rivers and farms of France. In Italy, you showed me the beautiful buildings of Naples and Venice, and the church in Padua that touches the heavens with the cross on its high roof. You've shown me many places, Mephistopheles, but [*looking around at the golden furniture and high, beautifully decorated walls and ceiling surrounding him*] what place is this? Have you, as I requested, brought me inside the walls of Rome?

MEPHISTOPHELES: Of course I have, Faustus. We're in the room where the Pope receives his most important guests. I thought you'd like to meet him and see how St Peter's Day is celebrated. You'll meet some of the most cheerful monks in the world!

FAUSTUS [*pausing thoughtfully*]: That sounds fun. But first I want you to make me disappear so that I can enjoy myself here even more.

MEPHISTOPHELES [*touching Faustus on the shoulder*]: So now, Faustus, you can do whatever you want – no one will see you.

[*To the sound of music, the Pope enters with the Cardinal of Lorraine and several Monks.*]

THE POPE: My lord of Lorraine, come nearer.

FAUSTUS: Hurry, or let the Devil stick in your throat!

THE POPE [*looking around, surprised*]: Who said that? [*He turns to the Monks, who are staring around anxiously*] Monks, find out who it was.

A MONK [*after looking around the room and discussing things with his colleagues*]: There's no one here, your Holiness.*

THE POPE [*taking a golden dish from the table and offering it to Lorraine*]: Here's some wonderful meat that the bishop of Milan sent me.

FAUSTUS [*smiling playfully*]: Thank you, sir. [*He takes the dish.*]

THE POPE [*staring with shock at the dish that seems to be moving around in mid-air*]: Who took that dish from me? Can't anyone see? [*Faustus quickly takes the dish from the room and returns empty-handed. The Pope sighs, takes another dish from the table and offers it to Lorraine.*] This was sent to me by the bishop of Florence.

FAUSTUS [*taking the dish*]: I'll have this one, too.

THE POPE [*shocked but trying to appear calm*]: Oh, no, not again! [*He takes a cup from the table and turns to Lorraine.*] My lord, I drink to your health.

---

* Your Holiness: the correct way of addressing the Pope

'Who took that dish from me?'

FAUSTUS [*taking the cup*]: And *I* drink to *yours*.

[*The Pope looks afraid and confused. Lorraine moves forward, trying to calm him.*]

LORRAINE: My lord, it may be a ghost from hell trying to ask you for forgiveness.

THE POPE [*uncertainly*]: Possibly. [*to the Monks, who are also looking anxious*] Brothers, prepare a song to defend us from the anger of this ghost. [*He makes the sign of the cross with his right hand on his chest.*]

FAUSTUS [*amused*]: Why are you crossing yourself? I'd advise you not to do that again. [*The Pope makes another sign of the cross.*] That's the second time you've done that. I'm giving you fair warning – don't do it again. [*The Pope makes another sign of the cross, and Faustus hits him on the side of his head. The Pope, Lorraine and the Monks all run away. Faustus laughs and turns to Mephistopheles.*] Come, Mephistopheles, what shall we do now?

MEPHISTOPHELES [*shaking his head with a sigh*]: I don't know. The monks will return and try to send us away with a religious song.

FAUSTUS [*singing playfully*]:
A religious song? A book and a bell
To send brave Faustus off to hell?
No. On this St Peter's Day
It is the monks who'll run away!

[*The Monks return.*]

MONK: Come, brothers, let's all sing bravely.
THE MONKS [*singing slowly*]:
Damned is the ghost who stole the meat.
This ghost has lost all hope.
Damned is the ghost who stole the wine.
And hit our good, wise, Pope.

[*Faustus and Mephistopheles attack the Monks, who run away. Faustus and Mephistopheles chase them, hitting them and laughing.*]

Scene 15 Robin and Rafe Meet Mephistopheles

[*A shadowy wood outside the university. Robin and Rafe enter, looking at the book of spells by lamplight.*]

ROBIN [*excitedly*]: Didn't I tell you, Rafe? With this book of Doctor Faustus's, all our troubles have ended. It's a wonderful treasure for two simple horse-keepers to have. Our horses will be unusually well-fed while we have this book. [*He finds a page with an interesting spell.*] Stand back, while I call the name of Lucifer. [*reading loudly*] 'In the name of Lucifer, the Prince of Darkness, let great Mephistopheles appear!'

[*Mephistopheles enters, dressed in black, his face in shadow. Rafe is afraid and hides behind Robin. Robin tries to look brave but is really as afraid as Rafe.*]

MEPHISTOPHELES [*angrily to himself*]: In the name of the Devil, at whose feet the most powerful kings in the world kiss the ground, these foolish people annoy me. I've come all the way from Constantinople* because these stupid boys called my name.

ROBIN: All the way from Constantinople? You've had a long journey. [*He takes a coin from his pocket and offers it to Mephistopheles.*] Will you take this to pay for your supper before you return?

MEPHISTOPHELES [*aiming his shining red eyes at Robin*]: Young man, for your brave stupidity, I'll change you into a cat. [*to Rafe*] And I'll change *you* into a dog. [*He leaves.*]

ROBIN [*with a foolish smile*]: Am I going to be a cat? That's good.

* Constantinople: the city now called Istanbul

Then I'll be able to catch birds in the highest trees.

RAFE [*suddenly looking pleased with himself*]: And I'm going to be a dog.

ROBIN [*laughing*]: With your ugly face never out of the soup-pot!

[*They leave, laughing.*]

Scene 16 The Storyteller Continues the Story

[*The Storyteller enters and stands in front of the curtain.*]

STORYTELLER: When Faustus had visited the courts of all the kings and seen the rarest treasures in the world, he returned home. His friends and colleagues, who had been worried about him, greeted his safe return with warm words of welcome. They listened with great wonder and admiration to his description of his journey around the world. Then they asked him questions about the secret mysteries of magic, which he answered with great intelligence and skill. He became famous across Europe, and is now at the palace of Carolus the Fifth, the King of Germany. Let us see what is happening there.

[*The Storyteller leaves and the curtain goes up.*]

Scene 17 Faustus Introduces a King to Alexander the Great

[*Several years have passed. Faustus, the King of Germany, and an important Army Officer are sitting around a table in a large room in the king's palace. They are enjoying a big meal. Mephistopheles, who is dressed again as a monk, stands quietly, unseen by the others, behind*]

Faustus's chair. Servants stand around the table. Faustus is looking much older now. His hair and beard are going grey.]

KING: Doctor Faustus, I've heard a lot about your great knowledge of the secrets of life. No one in the world is as skilled as you in the use of magic. They say that a powerful, mysterious spirit helps you to get whatever you want. This, therefore, is my request: prove your skill to me. Let my eyes witness what my ears have heard. I promise you that, whatever you do, you won't be criticised or punished.

ARMY OFFICER [*to the audience, with an amused smile*]: He looks like an ordinary magician to me.

FAUSTUS [*to the king, with an embarrassed smile*]: My lord, I'm much less skilful than people say, and much less powerful than a great man like you. But, with a sense of love and duty, I'm happy to obey every command you make.

KING: So, Faustus, listen to me carefully. Sometimes, when I sit alone in my room, I think about the kings and princes who lived and died before me. With their bravery and skill, they had great power, became very rich and won many wars. I sometimes worry that I'll never be as great as them. The most admired of all those kings must be Alexander the Great.*
The brightness of his shining life still lights our world today. Whenever I hear his name, I feel sad that I never met him. I want you, therefore, with your knowledge of the magic arts, to bring this great man back to life. I also want to see his beautiful queen. They must have the same appearance, character and dress as when they first lived in the past. If you can do that, you'll satisfy my desire and my opinion of you will be high.

FAUSTUS: My lord, I'll perform for you whatever the power of

* Alexander the Great: Alexander III, King of Macedon (336–323 BC), one of the most successful army commanders in history

my spirit will allow me.

ARMY OFFICER [*to the audience*]: In my opinion, he has no power of spirit at all.

FAUSTUS [*smiling nervously*]: Unfortunately, my lord, I don't have the power to bring back from the dead the real Alexander and his wife, whose bodies turned to dust long ago …

ARMY OFFICER [*laughing to the audience*]: Congratulations, Doctor. This honesty means that you're not completely bad.

FAUSTUS: … but I can bring you spirits that will look and behave exactly like them in every detail. I hope that this will satisfy you, my lord.

KING: Continue, Doctor Faustus. Let me see them immediately.

ARMY OFFICER [*to Faustus, with a look of amused disbelief*]: Do you know what you're saying, Doctor? Are you really going to make Alexander and his queen appear in front of our king?

FAUSTUS [*offended*]: Why not?

ARMY OFFICER [*laughing*]: If you can do that, then I'm a cow!

FAUSTUS: Don't laugh – you'll soon grow horns! [*He whispers over his shoulder to Mephistopheles.*] Mephistopheles, go now.

[*Mephistopheles leaves.*]

ARMY OFFICER [*who has heard Faustus speaking to Mephistopheles*]: No, you continue with your magic. *I'm* going! [*He stands up and leaves angrily.*]

FAUSTUS [*to himself*]: I'll make you pay for so rudely interrupting me. [*to the king*] Here they are, my lord.

[*Mephistopheles enters with Alexander the Great and his beautiful Persian Queen.*]

KING [*to Faustus*]: Doctor Faustus, I heard that, in real life, this lady had a red mark on her neck. How can I discover whether this is true?

FAUSTUS: You may go and see for yourself.

[*The King leaves the table and examines the Queen. As he returns to his seat, Alexander and his Queen leave.*]

KING [*with admiration*]: They were not spirits, but the real bodies of Alexander and his wife.

FAUSTUS: Would it be possible now, my lord, to send for the army officer who, a short time ago, was so unpleasant to me?

KING [*to a Servant*]: Fetch him back here. [*The Servant leaves and returns with the Army Officer, who has a pair of horns on his head.*] How are you, my good sir? I see that you've decided to grow horns on your head.

ARMY OFFICER [*surprised by the King's words, touching the horns on his head and staring angrily at Faustus*]: You son of the Devil, you evil dog! How dare you do this to a gentleman! I command you to take these horns away immediately!

FAUSTUS [*calmly*]: Not so fast, sir. Be patient. Have you forgotten already how you so rudely interrupted my conversation with the king? I think you've received a fair reward.

KING [*amused*]: Good Doctor Faustus, please take his horns away. I think he's been punished enough.

FAUSTUS: My lord, I gave this man horns for your amusement, not because he insulted me. I've succeeded in my aim, so now I'll gladly take his horns away. [*to the Army Officer*] In future, sir, speak more politely to scholars. [*to Mephistopheles*] Mephistopheles, take his horns away. [*The horns fall to the floor. Faustus stands up and turns to the king.*] Now, my lord, I've done my duty and must leave you.

KING [*standing up and offering Faustus his hand to kiss*]: Goodbye, Doctor Faustus. But before you go, you can expect a generous reward from me.

[*The King leaves with the Army Officer and his Servants.*]

FAUSTUS: Now, Mephistopheles, time continues its endless journey, and the end of my life is already coming into view.

I can't waste a moment, so let's hurry to Wittenberg. [*Wagner enters.*] So, Wagner, what news do you bring?

WAGNER: Sir, the Duke of Vanholt wants to see you urgently.

FAUSTUS: The Duke of Vanholt! A very important gentleman. I mustn't be shy with my special skills. [*to Mephistopheles*] Come, Mephistopheles, let's go to him immediately.

[*Faustus, Mephistopheles and Wagner leave.*]

Scene 18 Faustus Finds Grapes in Winter

[*A large room in the Duke of Vanholt's palace. The Duke and Duchess of Vanholt are sitting in large armchairs. The Duchess is clearly expecting a baby. Faustus is standing in front of them with Mephistopheles standing behind him. The Duke is laughing because Faustus has been entertaining him with his stories. The Duchess is smiling politely.*]

DUKE [*laughing*]: Believe me, Doctor Faustus, these stories are very entertaining.

FAUSTUS: My lord, I'm glad you enjoy them. [*to the Duchess*] But perhaps, madam, you don't like them so much? I've heard that women in your condition often have strange desires for special things. What would you like, madam? Tell me, and I'll get it for you.

DUCHESS: Thank you, good doctor. As you've so kindly offered to please me, I won't hide from you my heart's desire. Although it's January, the middle of winter, I'd love a dish of fresh grapes.

FAUSTUS [*smiling*]: That's no problem, madam. [*to Mephistopheles*] Go, Mephistopheles. [*Mephistopheles leaves.*] [*to the Duchess*] I'd be happy to get you whatever you want. [*Mephistopheles enters with a dish of grapes. Faustus takes the dish and offers it to the Duchess.*] Here they are, madam. Would you like to taste one?

[*The Duchess tastes the grapes.*]

DUKE: Believe me, good doctor, this is the greatest mystery of all. How did you manage to find fresh grapes at this time of year?

FAUSTUS: The world has different seasons at the same time of year. When it's winter for us, it's summer in countries further south. I've brought these grapes to you with the help of a fast-moving spirit. [*to the Duchess*] How do you like them, madam?

DUCHESS [*enthusiastically*]: They're the best grapes I've ever tasted.

FAUSTUS: I'm glad you like them.

DUKE [*taking the Duchess's hand as they both stand*]: Come, madam, let's go and eat. You must reward this clever man for the great kindness that he's shown you.

DUCHESS: Of course I will, my lord. I'll be eternally grateful to him.

FAUSTUS: Thank you, my lord and lady.

DUKE: Come, my good doctor; follow us and receive your reward.

[*They leave.*]

Scene 19 The Scholars Admire Helen of Troy

[*Twenty-four years have almost passed since Faustus signed his agreement with the Devil. Wagner, looking older, enters Faustus's study alone.*]

WAGNER: I think my master intends to die soon, because he's given me all his belongings. But if his death is so near, why is he drinking, eating and celebrating so much with his colleagues? Even as I speak, he's having more fun than I've ever seen him have before. [*There is the sound of loud voices and laughing.*] Look at him now – it seems that the meal's just ended.

[*Wagner leaves. Faustus enters with the three Scholars. Mephistopheles follows quietly.*]

FIRST SCHOLAR: Doctor Faustus, after our discussion about beautiful ladies, we decided that Helen of Troy* was the most beautiful woman who ever lived. Therefore, good doctor, we'd be very grateful if you could let us see her.

FAUSTUS: Gentlemen, you're good friends of mine, and I can't refuse your request. So I'll show you Helen when she was at her most beautiful – when Paris took her from Greece and crossed the seas with her to Troy.

[*There is the sound of music and Helen of Troy slowly crosses the stage. The three Scholars watch her, wide-eyed and open-mouthed with admiration and disbelief.*]

SECOND SCHOLAR: Words can't describe how beautiful she is.

THIRD SCHOLAR: I'm not surprised the Greeks fought a bloody war for ten years to get her back. Nothing on Earth or in the heavens is as beautiful as she was.

FIRST SCHOLAR: We've been lucky enough to see nature at its most heavenly and perfect. [*An Old Man enters.*] Before we go, let's wish Faustus eternal happiness for giving us such a wonderful, unforgettable experience.

FAUSTUS: Goodbye, gentlemen, and I wish the same for you.

[*The Scholars leave.*]

★ Helen of Troy: the daughter of Zeus, the king of the gods, and Leda, and the wife of Menelaus, King of Sparta. According to the Greek writer, Homer, in his famous poem *The Iliad*, Paris, a prince of Troy, stole her and started the ten-year Trojan War (12th century BC).

Scene 20 Faustus Receives a Final Warning

[*Faustus, Mephistopheles and the Old Man are in Faustus's study.*]

OLD MAN: Ah, Doctor Faustus, allow me to guide you along the path to eternal peace. You've done many evil things, the smell of which poisons your soul. You've lived a life of so much sin that only one thing can save you: God's forgiveness. Only His blood can wash away your guilt.

FAUSTUS [*crying to himself with self-pity*]: Where are you, Faustus? You sinful man, what have you done? You're damned, Faustus, damned! You deserve no pity – you must die! Hell's voice thunders in your ears: 'Faustus, your time has come!' [*Mephistopheles gives him a knife.*] And Faustus will obey hell's command.

[*Faustus prepares to push the knife into his own heart, but the Old Man stops him.*]

OLD MAN: Wait, Faustus. I can see an angel flying above you, inviting you to save your soul. Ask him for forgiveness.

FAUSTUS [*pausing, looking gratefully at the Old Man*]: Ah, my sweet friend, thank you for pitying my undeserving soul. But leave me – I need to think about my sins in private.

OLD MAN [*softly*]: All right, Faustus, but I'm leaving with a heavy heart. I'm worried that you're going to lose your soul. [*He leaves.*]

FAUSTUS [*to himself, confused*]: Proud Faustus, where's forgiveness now? I repent of my sins, but I feel no hope. Hell fights for control of my heart. What can I do to escape eternal death?

MEPHISTOPHELES [*angrily*]: You ungrateful man, Faustus. You should feel ashamed of disobeying my master in this way. Be strong, or I'll pull your body to pieces.

FAUSTUS [*ashamed of himself*]: Sweet Mephistopheles, ask your master to forgive my weakness. With my blood, I'll repeat the agreement that I made with Lucifer.

MEPHISTOPHELES [*spreading a document on the table and offering Faustus a pen*]: Then do it quickly, with a brave heart. You'll be in great danger if you delay.

[*Faustus cuts his arm with the knife, wets the pen with his blood and writes on the document.*]

FAUSTUS [*after writing on the document*]: Sweet friend, you must punish that dishonest old man who tried to turn me away from Lucifer. Punish him with all the pain that hell can offer.

MEPHISTOPHELES: His belief in God is great, and I can't touch his soul. But I'll cause his body as much pain as I can. It may not be very much.

FAUSTUS: Let me ask you for one thing, good servant, to satisfy the burning desire in my heart. If the heavenly Helen of Troy could be my lover, all thought of disloyalty to Lucifer would leave my mind.

MEPHISTOPHELES: Faustus, whatever you desire is yours.

[*Mephistopheles makes a sign with his hand and Helen appears.*]

FAUSTUS [*weak with desire for Helen as she walks towards him*]: Was this the face that caused a thousand ships to sail from Greece? Sweet Helen, make me live forever with a kiss. [*They kiss. Faustus is breathless with excitement.*] Her lips drink the soul from my body. See it fly! Come, Helen, give me my soul again. [*They kiss again.*] I never want to leave here, because there's heaven in her lips. Without Helen, everything else is meaningless. [*The Old Man returns, but Faustus continues talking to Helen.*] You're mine, and for your love I'll destroy Wittenberg, not Troy. I'll fight your weak husband, Menelaus, and all my other enemies, and then I'll return to Helen for a kiss. Oh, you're lovelier than the evening air dressed with a thousand stars. I want nothing in the world as much as you. [*He leaves with Helen and Mephistopheles.*]

'Was this the face that caused a thousand ships to sail from Greece?'

OLD MAN [*shaking his head sadly*]: Oh, Faustus, you foolish man. You've chased heaven from your soul and turned your back on God's forgiveness. [*Three Devils enter, dressed in black with burning eyes. They carry long forks and slowly surround the Old Man.*] Ah, Lucifer's come to challenge my belief in God. [*loudly to the Devils*] My love of God is stronger than my fear of you. You evil things, see how heaven defends me from you with a smile, and laughs in the face of your master in hell! Go back to your master, because I'm going to run to my God!

[*The Old Man is chased from the stage by the Devils.*]

Scene 21 Who Can Save Faustus?

[*Faustus, looking weak and ill, is sitting at the desk in his study. He is one hour away from his appointment with the Devil. The three Scholars enter.*]

FAUSTUS [*smiling weakly*]: Ah, gentlemen!

FIRST SCHOLAR [*to the Second Scholar, shocked by Faustus's appearance*]: What's the matter with Faustus?

FAUSTUS [*with a mad look in his eyes*]: Ah, my sweet colleagues, if I were living among you, I'd still be alive. But now I face eternal death. [*looking around nervously*] Look, he's coming, isn't he?

[*The Scholars speak among themselves.*]

SECOND SCHOLAR: What does Faustus mean?

THIRD SCHOLAR: His health's been affected by too much time alone.

FIRST SCHOLAR: If that's true, doctors can cure him. [*to Faustus*] Don't worry, Faustus. You probably just need a rest.

FAUSTUS [*bitterly*]: I need a rest from the deadly sins that have eaten my body and soul.

SECOND SCHOLAR: Faustus, look up to heaven. Remember, God's

forgiveness is eternal.

FAUSTUS: But my crime can never be forgiven. Ah, gentlemen, listen to me patiently, and don't be shocked by what I tell you. Not only Germany, but the whole world has witnessed the miracles that I've performed. But because of this, Faustus has lost Germany, the world, and even heaven itself. He must stay in hell forever! Sweet friends, what will happen to Faustus if he burns in the eternal flames of hell?

THIRD SCHOLAR: You can still ask God for help.

FAUSTUS: I've insulted God too much. I want to cry, but the Devil's stolen my tears. I'd cry blood instead of tears. Oh, he controls my tongue. I want to lift my hands – but look! They hold them down.

ALL [*anxiously*]: Who, Faustus?

FAUSTUS: Lucifer and Mephistopheles. Ah, gentlemen, in return for my miraculous powers, I gave them my soul.

ALL [*shocked*]: No, it can't be true!

FAUSTUS: I did it all against God's wishes. For the meaningless pleasure of twenty-four years, I've lost eternal peace and happiness. I wrote an agreement with my own blood. Now my time has come and the Devil's coming to fetch me.

FIRST SCHOLAR: Why didn't you tell us about this before?

FAUSTUS: I wanted to many times, but the Devil warned me not to. He said he'd destroy me if I talked about God. He'd take my body and soul if I listened to God's advice. And now it's too late. Gentlemen, you must leave immediately if you don't want to die with me.

SECOND SCHOLAR: Oh, what can we do to help you?

FAUSTUS: Don't think about me – save yourselves!

THIRD SCHOLAR: God will give me strength. I'll stay with Faustus.

FIRST SCHOLAR [*to the Third Scholar*]: Don't tempt God, sweet friend, but let's go into the next room and ask Him to save Faustus's soul.

FAUSTUS: You can try if you like, but nothing can save my soul.

SECOND SCHOLAR: Go on your knees and ask God to forgive you. We'll do the same.

FAUSTUS: Gentlemen, goodbye. If I'm still alive in the morning, I'll visit you. If not, then Faustus has gone to hell.

ALL: Goodbye, Faustus.

[*The Scholars leave. The clock strikes eleven o'clock.*]

Scene 22 Faustus Keeps His Appointment with the Devil

[*Faustus is alone in his study.*]

FAUSTUS: Ah, Faustus, you have only one hour to live and then you'll be damned to eternal hell. [*He opens his arms and looks up at the ceiling.*] Stop moving, all you stars in heaven. Stop all time, so that midnight never comes! Let this hour become a year or even just a month, a week, a natural day. With more time, I could repent and save my soul. [*sighing*] But the stars are still moving, time's running, the clock will strike and the Devil will come. And Faustus must be damned. Oh, I want to jump up to my God, but who's holding me down? Christ's blood streams across the heavens. One drop would save my soul – or even half a drop! [*He looks around bravely, challenging the shadows that are growing around him.*]

Yes, I've said the name of Christ – don't pull me to pieces for saying it. But I'll call his name again! [*falling to his knees*] Don't punish me, Lucifer. Look, God's stretching out his arm and turning His angry face towards me. [*He holds onto the desk for support.*] Mountains and hills, come fall on me. Hide me from the terrible anger of God. [*He hides under the desk and hits the*

44

floor with his hands.] Earth, open up and let me hide inside you. [*He sits up with a sigh.*] But I'll find no protection there. [*He moves out from under the desk, jumps to his feet and looks up at the ceiling.*] Or you – the stars that shone when I was born! Lift me up into a thundercloud. Destroy my body with your storm, but let my soul fly up to heaven. [*The clock strikes half past eleven.*]

Another thirty minutes – the end is near. Oh, God, even if you can't forgive me, let there be a limit to my pain. Let me live in hell for a thousand – or even a hundred thousand – years. But after that, let me be saved. [*sadly*] But the pain of a damned soul is endless. Oh, why couldn't I be an animal without a soul? All animals are happy because, when they die, their soulless bodies simply turn to dust. But my soul must burn forever in the fires of hell. [*angrily*] I hate my parents for giving birth to me! [*suddenly ashamed*] No, hate yourself, Faustus. Hate Lucifer, who has stolen from you the eternal happiness of heaven. [*The clock strikes midnight.*]

Oh, the end is here! Now, body, turn to air, or Lucifer will carry you off to hell. [*There is thunder and lightning. Faustus shouts.*] Oh, soul, change into little drops of water and fall into the ocean. The Devil will never find you there! [*He falls to his knees, his face filled with fear.*] Oh, God, don't look at me so angrily! [*Lucifer, Mephistopheles and other Devils enter.*] Let me breathe for a minute longer! Ugly hell, I'm not ready for you! [*Lucifer and Mephistopheles take him by the arms. Faustus fights, but without success. He screams as he is taken off to hell.*] Take your hands off me, Lucifer! I'll burn my books! Ah, Mephistopheles!

[*There is more thunder and lightning, and Faustus is taken away by the Devils. The curtain falls.*]

Scene 23 The Storyteller Brings the Story to an End

[*The Storyteller enters and stands in front of the curtain.*]

STORYTELLER: The curved branch did not grow straight and has been cut. Knowledge never became wise and has been burned. Faustus is gone. Be warned by his downfall. Hell often tempts the wise to admire unlawful things. They can seem attractive to our most intelligent minds. They can make us want to know more than heavenly power allows. But now, as the hour ends the day, the writer must end his work. [*The Storyteller leaves.*]

ACTIVITIES

Before you read

1 Discuss these questions with other students.

   a Which would you prefer: a short, exciting life or a long, boring one? Why?

   b In this story, a man has magical powers and can do whatever he wants. What would *you* do if you had magical powers?

2 Read the Introduction and answer these questions.

   a Match the names on the left with the correct description on the right:

John Faustus	a university
Wittenberg	the Devil
Lucifer	the Devil's helper
Mephistopheles	a famous scholar

   b Are these sentences about Christopher Marlowe true or false? (Correct the false ones.)

     1) He went to university with Shakespeare.

     2) He wrote five plays.

     3) He killed a man.

     4) He died in prison.

     5) He never saw *Dr Faustus* performed on stage.

3 Look at the Word List at the back of the book. Which words are for:

   a people?

   b feelings?

   c things that might or might not exist, depending on your beliefs?

While you read

4 Are these sentences about Faustus true (T) or false (F)?

   a His family was not rich. ....

   b He was born in Wittenberg. ....

   c He is a doctor of law. ....

   d He knows everything about magic. ....

   e He wants power and money. ....

47

f His friends warn him about the dangers of magic. ....

g His servant is a playful character. ....

h The two scholars are worried about him. ....

After you read

5 Which of these adjectives describe Faustus? Why?

    a intelligent   **d** satisfied

    b greedy   **e** excited

    c unpopular

6 How does Faustus feel about these subjects? Why?

    a philosophy   **d** theology

    b medicine   **e** magic

    c law

7 Work with another student. Have this conversation between Faustus and the head of the university.

    Student A: You are the head of the university. You think that magic is evil. Tell Faustus why.

    Student B: You are Faustus. You think that magic could make the world a better place. Tell the head of the university why.

8 Discuss these questions with another student.

    a Is philosophy important in today's world? Why / Why not?

    b Is Faustus mad? Why / Why not?

Scenes 5–8

Before you read

9 Discuss whether Faustus's new magic powers make him happy. Explain why / why not.

While you read

10 In which order do these things happen to Faustus? Number them 1–8.

    a He cuts his arm. ....

    b He learns about the Devil's past. ....

    c He gives Mephistopheles a signed agreement. ....

    d Mephistopheles appears to him for the first time. ....

e	He is visited by two female devils.	....
f	Mephistopheles warns him to change his mind.	....
g	He is visited by two angels.	....
h	He draws a circle on the ground.	....

After you read

11 How are these important in this part of the story?

  a water

  b twenty-four years

  c a bag of coins

  d blood

  e a bucket of burning wood

  f jewels and beautiful clothes

12 How do these people feel and why?

  a Faustus, when he first sees Mephistopheles.

  b Faustus, after the ugly shape leaves.

  c Faustus, after Mephistopheles first talks to him.

  d Mephistopheles, after describing hell to Faustus.

  e Mephistopheles, when Faustus sends him back to Lucifer with a message.

  f Robin, when Wagner talks about the devil.

  g Faustus, while he is waiting for Mephistopheles to return.

  h Faustus, after the angels leave.

  i Faustus, when he sees the sign on his arm.

  j Faustus, after the female devils leave.

13 Discuss these questions with other students. What do you think?

  a Why does Faustus want Mephistopheles to look like a monk?

  b According to Mephistopheles, why did he come to Faustus?

  c If you were Robin, would you accept Wagner's offer? Why / Why not?

  d Why is Faustus worried while he is waiting for Mephistopheles to return in Scene 7? What changes his mind?

Scenes 9–12

Before you read

14 Discuss these questions with another student.

  a What will Faustus's first request be, do you think?

  b If you were Faustus, what would *your* first request be? Why?

While you read

15 Complete these sentences.

  a Faustus's .... belongs to Lucifer.

  b Faustus wants Mephistopheles to find him a ....

  c Faustus wants a book that will show him all the world's spells, the meaning of the .... and all the world's plants and trees.

  d .... steals one of Faustus's books.

  e The Good Angel tells Faustus to ....

  f Faustus has been visited by great writers and .... from the past.

  g .... introduces Faustus to the Seven Deadly Sins.

  h Faustus is given books by Mephistopheles and ....

After you read

16 Choose the correct ending to each of these sentences.

  a Faustus is not afraid of hell because he ...

  b Mephistopheles is surprised that Faustus ...

  c Faustus looks sick because he ...

  d There will be wild winds if Faustus ...

  e Faustus will have an army of loyal soldiers if he ...

  f Robin is excited because he ...

  g Faustus gets angry because Mephistopheles ...

  h Lucifer feels insulted because Faustus ...

  i Covetousness would be happy if everything ...

  j Jealousy would be happy if everyone ...

    1) draws a circle on the ground.

    2) hopes to see pretty girls dancing.

    3) refuses to answer a question.

    4) turned to gold.

    5) wants a wife.

50

6) finds his 'wife' very unattractive.

7) has used the name of Christ.

8) says some words three times.

9) died of hunger.

10) does not believe in it.

17 Discuss these questions with other students.

   a What does Faustus enjoy most about his agreement with the Devil in this part of the story? What does he like least? Why?

   b What does Mephistopheles refuse to tell Faustus? Why?

Scenes 13–18

Before you read

18 What will happen to Robin and Rafe? Why? Discuss your answers with other students.

While you read

19 Tick (✔) the correct answer.

   a In Greece, Faustus

     1) makes maps of the stars. ....

     2) meets the Pope. ....

     3) admires a tall church. ....

   b The Pope believes that Faustus might be a(n)

     1) spirit. ....

     2) angel. ....

     3) evil monk. ....

   c After their meeting with Mephistopheles, Robin and Rafe are

     1) afraid. ....

     2) thoughtful. ....

     3) amused. ....

   d When Faustus returns to Germany, he is

     1) criticised. ....

     2) celebrated. ....

     3) punished. ....

   e The King of Germany believes that Faustus

     1) is less skilful than people say. ....

     2) is as great as Alexander. ....

      3) has brought Alexander the Great back from the
         dead. ....

f Faustus punishes the army officer for his
    1) violent behaviour. ....
    2) bad eating habits. ....
    3) rudeness. ....

g Faustus tells the Duke of Vanholt that the grapes came from
    1) heaven. ....
    2) hell. ....
    3) another country. ....

After you read

20 What problems do these people have in this part of the story?
  a the Pope   **d** the army officer
  b the monks   **e** Faustus
  c Robin and Rafe   **f** Mephistopheles

21 Put these words in the right order and finish these sentences.
Who says or thinks these words? What are they talking about?
  a 'I want *to / me / disappear / make / you*.'
  b 'Brothers, prepare a song *anger / us / this / to / from / of / defend / the / ghost*.'
  c 'It's a *two / have / for / treasure / horse-keepers / to / simple / wonderful*.'
  d 'I heard that, in real life, *had / neck / this / mark / lady / red / on / a / her*.'
  e I command you *these / immediately / take / to / you / horns / away*!'
  f 'How did you *year / grapes / manage / this / at / time / to / fresh / find / of*?'

22 In groups of five, imagine and act out this scene. The characters are:

    the Pope   the army officer   the King of Germany
    the Duke of Vanholt   Robin

A world organization thinks that Faustus should receive its top
international prize for his services to science. Do you agree?
Make short speeches and then have a discussion.

Scenes 19–23

Before you read

23 Discuss these questions with other students.

    a How will Faustus feel as he nears the end of his twenty-four years? Why?

    b Will this story have a happy or a sad ending for Faustus? Why?

While you read

24 Who is speaking? Who are they speaking to?

    a 'You're good friends of mine, and I can't refuse your request.'

    .... / ....

    b 'I can see an angel flying above you.'

    .... / ....

    c 'You ungrateful man.'

    .... / ....

    d 'Make me live forever with a kiss.'

    .... / ....

    e 'My love of God is stronger than my fear of you.'

    .... / ....

    f 'Don't think about me – save yourselves!'

    .... / ....

    g 'Let there be a limit to my pain.'

    .... / ....

    h 'Take your hands off me … !'

    .... / ....

After you read

25 In his last speech, the Storyteller explains the lesson that can be learnt from Faustus's story. What is that lesson? Explain it in your own words.

26 Discuss these questions with other students.

    a What do you think of Faustus's treatment of the old man? What does this tell you about his character?

    b In the whole story, which of the seven Deadly Sins is Faustus guilty of?

53

Writing

27 Faustus would like to make men live forever (Scene 2). Would you like to live forever? Write about the advantages and disadvantages.

28 Imagine that you are one of the Scholars (Scene 4). Write a letter to the head of the university explaining why you are worried about Faustus.

29 Look at Scene 12 again. Which is the worst deadly sin, in your opinion? Which is the least serious? Why? Which deadly sin are *you* most guilty of?

30 Imagine that you are a reporter at the Pope's palace (Scene 14). Write about the scene for your newspaper under the title, 'Is the Pope Going Mad?'

31 Imagine that you are Robin (Scene 15). Write a letter to your parents, explaining how and why you have changed into cat.

32 If you could meet one famous person from history, who would it be? Why? What questions would you ask him / her? Write your conversation.

33 Imagine that you are Faustus (Scene 21). Send God a letter of repentance. Tell him why you deserve to be saved from eternal hell.

34 Imagine that you are Lucifer. Mephistopheles has left you and you need a new assistant. Write a job description. Make the job sound as interesting and rewarding as possible.

36 If you had Faustus's magic powers for twenty-four years, how would you use them? Write about it for a college magazine.

37 What lessons can we learn from this story today?

Answers for the Activities in this book are available from the Pearson English Readers website. A free Activity Worksheet is also available from the website. Activity worksheets are part of the Pearson English Readers Teacher Support Programme, which also includes Progress tests and Graded Reader Guidelines. For more information, please visit: www.pearsonenglishreaders.com

WORD LIST

angel (n) a spirit, especially with wings, who is believed to live with God in heaven

audience (n) the people in a theatre who watch a play

bishop (n) the most important church official in a city

cardinal (n) a person with a very high position in the Catholic church

challenge (n/v) something new, exciting or difficult that needs a lot of skill to do

covetousness (n) a strong desire for something that belongs to someone else

damned (adj) sent to eternal hell after death as punishment by God; this is a state of **damnation**

devil (n) a spirit from hell; **the Devil** is God's most powerful enemy

downfall (n) a situation when you suddenly lose success, importance or money

duke / duchess (n) a man / woman with the highest social position below a prince and princess

eternal (adj) continuing for ever

evil (n/adj) something very bad, with a cruel or harmful effect

grape (n) a small, round, juicy fruit, usually green or purple, from which wine is produced

horn (n) one of the two hard, pointed parts that grows on the heads of some animals (for example, cows)

lust (n) very strong sexual desire

master (n/v) the male employer of a servant, or the governor of an area. If you **master** a subject, you know everything about it.

miracle (n) a good action or event that seems impossible, and is **miraculous**

monk (n) a member of a group of religious men who live together

philosophy (n) the study of ideas about existence

pride (n) the feeling of being proud

repent (v) to be sorry for something that you have done

scholar (n) someone who studies a subject and knows a lot about it

sigh (n/v) a heavy breath out, showing that you are tired, bored or annoyed

sin (n/v) bad actions that religious laws do not allow; there are traditionally seven **deadly sins**

soul (n) the part of you that continues to exist after your death

spell (n) special words that are used to make magic happen

spirit (n) a living thing without a physical body

tempt (v) to make someone want to have something, although it might be wrong

theology (n) the study of religion

treasure (n) a collection of gold, silver and jewels, especially when they are hidden